Macmillan English

Fluency Book

3

Mary Bowen

Louis Fidge

Liz Hocking

Wendy Wren

MACMILLAN

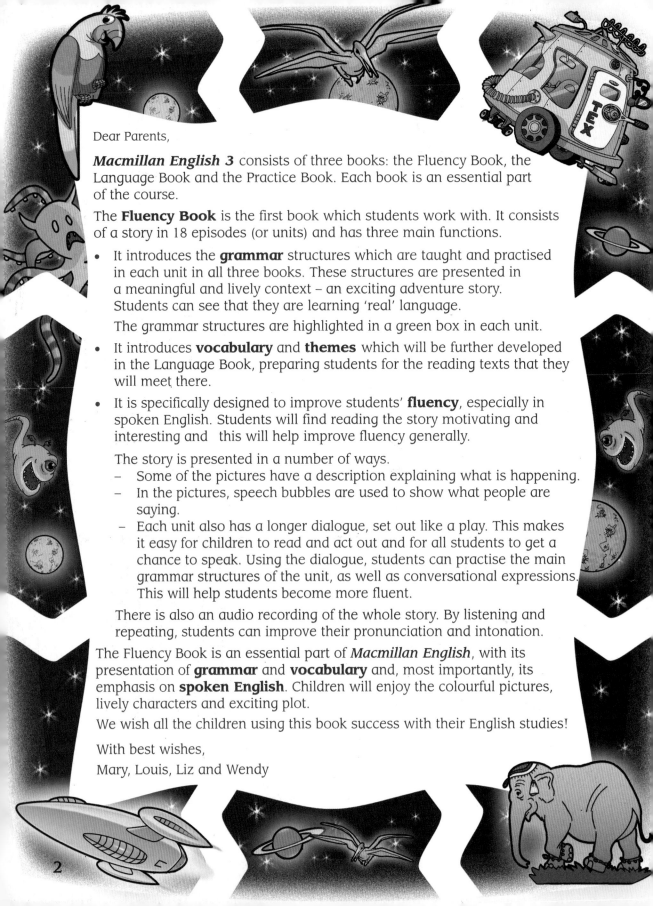

Dear Parents,

Macmillan English 3 consists of three books: the Fluency Book, the Language Book and the Practice Book. Each book is an essential part of the course.

The **Fluency Book** is the first book which students work with. It consists of a story in 18 episodes (or units) and has three main functions.

- It introduces the **grammar** structures which are taught and practised in each unit in all three books. These structures are presented in a meaningful and lively context – an exciting adventure story. Students can see that they are learning 'real' language.

  The grammar structures are highlighted in a green box in each unit.

- It introduces **vocabulary** and **themes** which will be further developed in the Language Book, preparing students for the reading texts that they will meet there.

- It is specifically designed to improve students' **fluency**, especially in spoken English. Students will find reading the story motivating and interesting and   this will help improve fluency generally.

  The story is presented in a number of ways.
  - Some of the pictures have a description explaining what is happening.
  - In the pictures, speech bubbles are used to show what people are saying.
  - Each unit also has a longer dialogue, set out like a play. This makes it easy for children to read and act out and for all students to get a chance to speak. Using the dialogue, students can practise the main grammar structures of the unit, as well as conversational expressions. This will help students become more fluent.

  There is also an audio recording of the whole story. By listening and repeating, students can improve their pronunciation and intonation.

The Fluency Book is an essential part of *Macmillan English*, with its presentation of **grammar** and **vocabulary** and, most importantly, its emphasis on **spoken English**. Children will enjoy the colourful pictures, lively characters and exciting plot.

We wish all the children using this book success with their English studies!

With best wishes,

Mary, Louis, Liz and Wendy

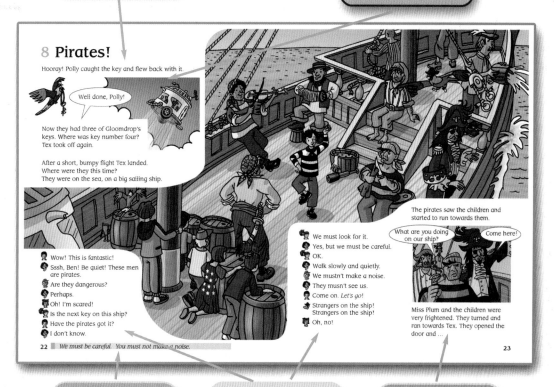

Narrative text sets the scene for this unit.

Small pictures and speech bubbles move the story along.

8 Pirates!

Hooray! Polly caught the key and flew back with it.

Well done, Polly!

Now they had three of Gloomdrop's keys. Where was key number four? Tex took off again.

After a short, bumpy flight Tex landed. Where were they this time? They were on the sea, on a big sailing ship.

Wow! This is fantastic!
Sssh, Ben! Be quiet! These men are pirates.
Are they dangerous?
Perhaps.
Oh! I'm scared!
Is the next key on this ship?
Have the pirates got it?
I don't know.

We must look for it.
Yes, but we must be careful.
OK.
Walk slowly and quietly.
We mustn't make a noise.
They mustn't see us.
Come on. *Let's go!*
Strangers on the ship! Strangers on the ship!
Oh, no!

The pirates saw the children and started to run towards them.

What are you doing on our ship?

Come here!

Miss Plum and the children were very frightened. They turned and ran towards Tex. They opened the door and …

22 ▌ *We must be careful. You must not make a noise.*

23

The important grammar structures of the unit are clearly shown at the bottom of the first page.

The main dialogue of the unit is presented as a play. It contains examples of the grammar structures, conversational phrases and expressions which will help fluency.

The unit ends with narrative text which encourages interest in the next episode of the story.

Gloomdrop

Princess Starlight

Miss Plum

Polly

Jack

Tilly

Nina

Sam

Mobi

Ben

4

Tex the time explorer machine

On Monday morning Sam, Ben, Nina and Tilly were at school. At nine o'clock they had an English lesson with their teacher, Miss Plum. They walked to her classroom but they did not go inside. There was a sign on the door. 'That's very strange,' said Tilly. 'What is Miss Plum doing in there?'

Ben and Nina jumped up and down. They tried to look into the room. Sam and Mobi listened at the door. What were those strange noises? What was in the room?

1 This is Tex

Miss Plum opened the classroom door and the children went inside. There was a strange machine in the classroom. What was it?

This is Tex. It's my time explorer machine.

We're not having an English lesson today. We're going on a trip through time.

Fantastic!

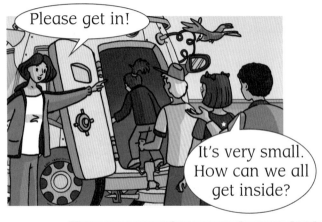

Please get in!

It's very small. How can we all get inside?

Outside the time machine looked very small. Inside it was very big!

Welcome to Tex!

Wow!

It's huge!

Look at all these lights!

Look at all these buttons and dials!

Look at the handle and the switches!

They are the controls. Don't touch them!

What's this, Miss Plum?

This is the computer.

It was ...   She opened ...   It looked ...

 Look! There's a message on the screen.

What does it say?

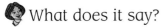 It says: 'Help! Help!'

'I am Princess Starlight from planet Smilo.'

'Please, please, help me!'

Come on, children. Take your seats!
We're going to planet Smilo!

Now?

Now.

Wow!

5 – 4 – 3 – 2 – 1 ...

Here we go!

2 Up in space

The children and Miss Plum were in Tex, the time explorer machine. Soon they were high above the earth. They looked out of the windows. They saw stars and planets.

They saw some strange creatures too.
One creature had two heads with horns and long purple arms.
Another creature had huge orange wings and green paws with claws.
Another creature had one large red eye, a big mouth, sharp teeth and scales.

Suddenly they heard a strange noise. It was the computer.

 Look! There's a picture on the screen.

 I think it's Princess Starlight.

 There's a message too.

 What does it say? Can you read it?

 It says: 'The children on planet Smilo were very happy.'

 'They played games and laughed all day long.'

 'Yesterday Gloomdrop came to our planet'.

 'He's a very bad creature.'

He took ... They saw ... It had ... They heard ... He hid ...

'Here is his photo.' Oooh!

'He took the laughter from the children.'

'He put it in a big box.'

'He locked the box with nine keys.'

'Then he hid the keys in different places and times.'

'Now the children can't laugh.'

'They are sad all day long.'

'You have a time machine.'

'Please help us to find the keys.'

3 The first key

Tex, the time machine, went round and round and up and down.

It jumped to the right and bumped to the left ...

... and then it stopped.

Miss Plum opened the door and looked outside. It was very dark.

Miss Plum and the children went outside. They were in a big, dark cave. It was very, very quiet. Miss Plum walked in front. The children walked behind her in a line.

Did you see ... ?   I did not see ...

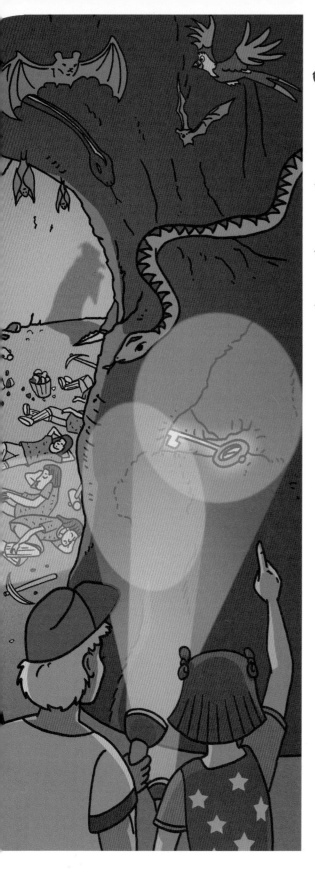

Look at those men! Who are they?

I don't know.

Sshh! They're sleeping.

Oh! Did you see that?

What?

It was an eye, a red eye shining in the dark.

I didn't see anything.

Look over there.

You're right! A red eye ... and a blue eye ... and two green eyes.

They aren't eyes. They're jewels!

Wow! There are jewels everywhere.

What's that?

It's a key. A gold key!

♪♫♪♫♪

Be quiet, Mobi!

Oh no! The men are waking up!

I'm scared!

Quick! Let's go back to Tex!

Run!

Is this a key to Gloomdrop's box?

Miss Plum and the children were back in Tex.
It was time to go – but where to?

13

4 In the desert

The children had one key to Gloomdrop's box.
Where were the other keys?

Tex landed with a bump.

Miss Plum opened the door and
they all went outside.

Where are we now?

Where were they? The land was flat and dry and brown.
Were they in the past, the present or the future?

Where are we, Miss Plum?

Well, I think we're in a desert.

A desert?

But deserts are hot, aren't they?

This place isn't hot.

Brrr! The wind is as cold as ice.

And deserts are sandy, aren't they?

This place is rocky.

as cold as ... longer than ...

Far away they saw a cloud of dust.
It came nearer and nearer.

Oh! What are they?

Are they cows?

No. They're called yaks.

Look at their horns!

They're as long as my arms.

They're longer than your arms!

Look over there! What is it?

I don't know.

What was it?

15

5 Yorgi's house

The cloud of dust stopped and they saw a young man on a camel. Behind him there were two more camels.

Yorgi's house was a big, round tent. They got off the camels and went inside.

Hello! My name is Yorgi. Please come with me to my house.

Thank you.

They all climbed on to Yorgi's camels.

These camels are very fast.

They are the fastest camels in the desert.

Soon they came to Yorgi's house.

This is my house.

Welcome to my house!

Thank you, Yorgi. It's beautiful.

It's very cosy and warm.

What colourful rugs and cushions!

What do you do here in the desert, Yorgi?

I look after my camels.

The fastest camels in the desert!

Yes. And I look after my yaks.

With the longest horns in the world!

the fastest ... the longest ... in the world

Yorgi, what's that round your neck?

I don't know. I found it under a rock in the desert.

Is it a key?

It's very strange, isn't it?

Do you like it?

Yes, I do.

Please take it. It's a present from the desert.

Thank you, Yorgi.

Is it a key to Gloomdrop's box?

Yes, I think it is.

The children and Miss Plum sat by the stove. Yorgi brought them bowls of warm milk. Then it was time to go back to Tex.

Goodbye!

They had two of Gloomdrop's keys. Where was the next one?

6 A very long time ago

Tex landed with a bump. The children opened the door and went outside. Where were they this time?

WHAT?

Were they in the present, the past or the future? They were all very, very surprised.

What's that?

Is it an elephant?

No, it's bigger than an elephant.

And it's more dangerous. It's a mammoth.

Wow! The men are hunting it!

This place is more exciting than the desert!

I think it's frightening.

It's the most frightening place ever!

more dangerous than … the most frightening … It is better … It is worse …

Look! There's another animal!

It's a huge tiger. Look at its teeth!

Oh! It's worse than the mammoth!

It's OK, Tilly. Don't be frightened.

Look! They're all running away into the forest.

Phew! That's better.

♩ ♪ ♩ ♪ ♪ ♩

What's the matter, Mobi?

Oh! Look!

A strange silver spaceship appeared on the path in front of them.

A beautiful young woman came out of the spaceship. Who was she?

7 The big balloon

Who got out of the spaceship? It was Princess Starlight!

My dear friends! Thank you for helping me!

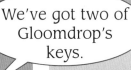

We've got two of Gloomdrop's keys.

Wonderful!

Princess Starlight got into her spaceship and disappeared.

Now I'm going back to Smilo. The children are so sad!

Goodbye!

The children and Miss Plum got into Tex. Off they went again – but where to?

Bump!

Tex landed in the corner of a green field. The sky was blue and the sun was hot. There was a huge crowd of people in the field but nobody saw Tex.

Well, children. We're in France and the year is 1793.

How do you know, Miss Plum?

Do you see that balloon?

Yes.

It's very famous.

Really?

You're going to see something fantastic.

What's going to happen, Miss Plum?

The balloon is going to rise up high in the sky.

You are going to see … It is going to rise up …

Look! There it goes!

Oh! It's beautiful!

That is the first hot air balloon. And those are the first passengers.

Oh! I can see a duck, a cockerel and a sheep!

That's funny!

Look! Something is falling from the balloon.

What is it?

Is it a key?

Go on, Polly!

You can do it!

Look at Polly! She's flying fast towards the balloon. Is she going to catch the key?

8 Pirates!

Hooray! Polly caught the key and flew back with it.

Well done, Polly!

Now they had three of Gloomdrop's keys. Where was key number four? Tex took off again.

After a short, bumpy flight Tex landed.
Where were they this time?
They were on the sea, on a big sailing ship.

Wow! This is fantastic!

Sssh, Ben! Be quiet! These men are pirates.

Are they dangerous?

Perhaps.

Oh! I'm scared!

Is the next key on this ship?

Have the pirates got it?

I don't know.

We must be careful. You must not make a noise.

The pirates saw the children and started to run towards them.

We must look for it.

Yes, but we must be careful.

OK.

Walk slowly and quietly.

We mustn't make a noise.

They musn't see us.

Come on. *Let's go*!

Strangers on the ship! Strangers on the ship!

Oh, no!

What are you doing on our ship?

Come here!

Miss Plum and the children were very frightened. They turned and ran towards Tex. They opened the door and …

9 Jack

Miss Plum and the children got inside Tex just in time!
The pirates banged on the door and shouted.

It's time to leave!

Come here!

Shut the door!

That was frightening!

Aaa - choo!

Who was that?

It was me!

Who are you?

My name's Jack.

You were on the pirate ship.

Yes. Gloomdrop put me there.

Oh! He's a bad, bad creature.

Why are you here in our time machine?

Because I don't want to live on the pirate ship. I want to go home.

We can't take you home.

We're travelling through time.

Why … ? Because … I want to go home.

We're looking for the keys to Gloomdrop's box.

Oh, please take me with you. Please take me home.

Where is your home?

It's on planet Smilo.

Really? We're going there!

Is your family on Smilo?

Yes. Take me with you. Please!

Can he come with us, Miss Plum?

Yes, of course.

The children were very happy. Only Tilly was a bit sad.

We didn't find the fourth key.

I've got a key! I found it on the ship.

Hooray!

25

10 What a trip!

Tex, the time machine, was travelling through time and space. Miss Plum was in the pilot's seat. The children were talking to Jack, the boy from the pirate ship. He wanted to know all about their journey in Tex. Nina showed him pictures of their trip on the computer.

Where did you go first?

First we went to a dark cave.

It was full of jewels.

They were shining in the dark.

Then we went to a cold desert.

We met a man called Yorgi.

He was riding a camel.

The next place was scary.

We saw a mammoth.

Really?

Some men were hunting it.

We met Princess Starlight there.

Then we went to France.

We saw the first hot air balloon.

It was beautiful.

Then we arrived on a pirate ship.

We saw a boy there.
He was dancing.

Who was that?

You, silly!

He was riding ...   They were hunting ...

27

11 Under the sea

Tex landed with a bump and a splash. Miss Plum and the children looked out of the windows.

The sea was clear and warm. Nina and Ben swam to some rocks. Miss Plum, Sam and Tilly swam to some coral. Tiny fish were swimming among its branches. But suddenly Miss Plum was worried. Where were Nina and Ben? Were they lost?

Miss Plum had diving suits for the children. They put them on and followed Miss Plum into the water. Jack and Polly stayed in Tex.

Miss Plum swam to the left. Tilly and Sam followed her but Nina and Ben swam to the right.

While you were having fun, I was worrying about you.

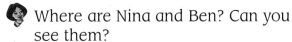 Where are Nina and Ben? Can you see them?

They're over there, Miss Plum. By the rocks.

Ben! Nina! Come here at once!

Here we are, Miss Plum.

What were you doing over there?

We were having fun!

Well, while you were having fun, I was worrying about you.

Sorry, Miss Plum.

We must all stay together.

Were you playing in the rocks?

Yes, we were.

What were you doing?

We were looking at the coral.

I saw a sea snake.

I found a starfish.

I want to see a shark.

Really?

Yes.

Well ... Look behind you!

A huge shark was swimming towards them.

Help!

12 The wreck

The big shark was swimming after the children. They were very frightened but Miss Plum was not worried.

Don't worry! This shark isn't dangerous.

Suddenly the children saw something in front of them.

What is it?

Is it a house?

No. It's a ship.

Wow! Come on!

The children swam round the wreck. It was a big, old ship.Then they swam into the wreck. What was inside?

 What can you see?

 There's nothing here.

 Only fish and crabs and – oh!

 What is it?

 It's a chest, an old chest.

 Wow!

 Can you open it?

 Ooh! No, I can't.

Can you open it? She could not open it.

Together they opened the chest.
It was full of gold coins.

Wow!

And under the coins there was ...

... a key!

Hooray!

Hello! Hello!

Who is it?

It's Miss Plum.

Oh! There you are! I couldn't find you.

Miss Plum! Nina found a chest.

Really?

But she couldn't open it.

Well, let's try all together. 1, 2, 3 ...

13 The flower seller

Back in Tex the children looked at the keys. They had five keys to Gloomdrop's box. They needed four more. Then they could open the box. Where was the next key?

Tex landed. Miss Plum opened the door and they looked outside.

We're in London. But it's London a long time ago.

They saw a girl. She was selling flowers. She looked sad. She was shivering with cold.

The street was busy but there were not any cars or buses or lorries. There were horses and carriages! They crossed the street and spoke to the girl.

Hello.

Hello.

Are you all right?

Yes, thank you. But the wind is so cold. And I'm hungry and thirsty too.

Oh dear!

I've got some chocolate.

And there's some juice in my flask.

Here you are.

Mmm! Delicious! Thank you.

You're welcome.

There is some juice. There were not any cars.

Who are you? Where do you come from?

We come from far away.

What are you doing here?

We're looking for a key.

A big key.

Really? That's very strange!

Why?

Because I found a big key this morning.

Where did you find it?

It was in my basket under the flowers.

Here it is!

The girl gave them the key. The children thanked her and said goodbye. They went back to Tex and took off again. Where were they going this time?

14 The chariot race

Where was Tex this time? The sky was blue and the sun was shining brightly. It was very hot. They were in a huge stadium and there were lots of people there. The people were shouting and clapping and cheering. Nobody noticed Tex, Miss Plum or the children because they were all watching … a chariot race!

A black chariot and a white chariot were racing round the stadium. Beautiful horses were pulling them.

We're in Rome a long time ago!

Listen to the crowd!

Look at the chariots and the horses!

Wow! They're going so fast!

I can't see. How many chariots are there?

There are two.

This is fantastic, isn't it?

Can we stay all day?

How much time have we got, Miss Plum?

I have no idea.

How many chariots are there? How much time have we got?

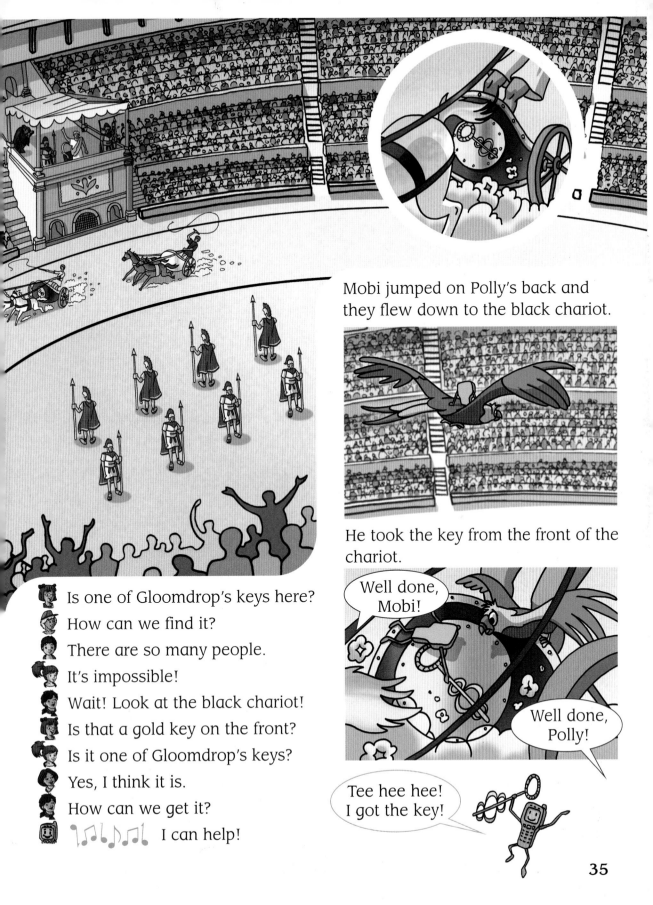

Mobi jumped on Polly's back and they flew down to the black chariot.

He took the key from the front of the chariot.

Well done, Mobi!

Well done, Polly!

Tee hee hee! I got the key!

Is one of Gloomdrop's keys here?

How can we find it?

There are so many people.

It's impossible!

Wait! Look at the black chariot!

Is that a gold key on the front?

Is it one of Gloomdrop's keys?

Yes, I think it is.

How can we get it?

I can help!

35

15 Be careful, Mobi!

Tex was travelling through space. The children were looking out of the windows.

What can you see, children?

I can see a planet.

That's planet Yum Yum.

What a funny name!

The planet is made of ice cream.

Mmm! I love ice cream.

The ice cream on Yum Yum is wonderful. It's all the colours of the rainbow.

I can see a planet. The planet is made of ice cream.

Miss Plum opened the door and the children picked crystals from the tree with nets.

Be careful, Nina!

Be very careful, Mobi!

Mobi was not careful. He slipped and fell.

Mobi! Where are you?

Help!

We can see birds.

They're very strange.

The birds at home have got two wings.

The birds here in space have got four wings!

Look over there! I can see a tree.

That's the crystal tree.

Oh, yes! There are lots of crystals.

They're hanging from its branches.

Do you want to pick some crystals?

Oh, yes, please!

He fell
down
down
down
down

16 Mobi and the crystals

Where was Mobi? Miss Plum flew Tex round and round and up and down but they could not see him.

Polly asked the strange birds.

Where is Mobi? Do you know?

Go to Yum Yum.

They flew to planet Yum Yum and found Mobi. He was lying in the ice cream. He was very happy.

Planet Yum Yum is yummy!

Sam threw a rope to him ...

Catch!

... and they pulled him up.

Are you all right, Mobi?

Yes, I'm fine.

You're a very naughty mobile.

I'm never naughty!

Oh yes, you are.

You always do something silly.

Not always!

Well ... sometimes.

You sometimes swing on the time dial.

Yes, I do. Sorry, Miss Plum.

always never sometimes

The crystals are beautiful.

They're fantastic.

Can I see them?

Yes, of course, Mobi.

Can I hold them?

Well, I don't know.

Please!

All right. But be careful!

OK.

This is fun!

Oh, no!

Mobi!

Look! That's key number eight!

Hooray!

39

17 A clever elephant

Tex landed with a bump. They were in a garden. There were trees and flowers. There was a pool with a fountain. It was beautiful but it was not a happy place. They saw some children. They were sitting quietly under the trees. Their faces were sad.

Look at those children!

What's the matter with them?

They aren't playing or laughing.

Why are they sad?

I know! This is planet Smilo!

Princess Starlight! Hello!

You're here at last.

Your planet is very beautiful.

It was more beautiful – and happier too – before Gloomdrop.

Can I talk to the children? Can we play with them?

Suddenly the elephant reached up its trunk. It wanted to pick an orange.

But it did not pick an orange. There in its trunk was a large, gold key!

Can I talk to the children?

Can we play with them?

No, they don't want to play.

They are all so sad.

They can't smile. They can't laugh.

Have you got the keys to Gloomdrop's box?

We've got eight keys.

We need one more.

We must find it!

It's the last key!

Now we can open the box!

Hooray!

18 Gloomdrop's box

Princess Starlight walked into her palace. She was carrying a purple cushion and on the cushion were the nine keys to Gloomdrop's box.

They walked into a large, beautiful room. In the middle of the room there was a table and on the table there was a big black box. The box had nine silver keyholes.

 Is that Gloomdrop's box?

 Yes, it is.

 It's very big, isn't it?

 I don't like it. It's scary.

 Is the children's laughter inside?

 Yes, it is.

 Look at the keys!

 They're shining more brightly.

 My key's shining the most brightly!

 Sssh, Mobi! Princess Starlight is going to speak.

 My dear friends, you are all holding a key.

 Can we open the box now?

 No! Wait!

 Please put your keys in the keyholes.

 Can I turn my key now?

 We're going to turn our keys all together. Are you ready?

 Yes!

One ... two ... three ...

They're shining more brightly. My key's shining the most brightly.

They all turned their keys and the black box opened. Laughter flew out of the box ...

Ho ho!

Ha ha!

Hee hee!

Ha ha ha!

Ha ha!

Tee hee hee!

Ha ha ha!

... and the children of planet Smilo were happy again.

We're smiling again.
We're laughing again.
Thank you for helping us. Thank you!
We're playing again.
We're dancing again.
Thank you for helping us. Thank you!

Goodbye! Goodbye!
Come back and see us soon!
Goodbye! Goodbye!
Come back and see us soon!
G-O-O-D-B-Y-E
Goodbye!

45

The nine keys

Wordlist

Pages 2–7: classroom, lesson, Monday, morning, noise, sign, teacher; strange; inside, up and down; listen (-ed), look (-ed), jump (-ed), say (said), try (tried).

Keep out!

Unit 1: button, computer, controls, dial, explorer, handle, light, machine, message, planet. princess, screen, switch, time, trip; huge; outside; get in, go (went), open (-ed), say, touch.

Come on! Fantastic! Help! Here we go! Take your seats! Welcome to...! Wow!

Unit 2: arm, box, children, claw, creature, earth, eye, game, head, horn, key, laughter, leg, paw, photo, picture, planet, scales, space, star, teeth, window, wing; bad, different, happy, sad; all day long, suddenly; come (came), find, have (had), hear (heard), hide (hid), laugh (-ed), lock (-ed), play (-ed), put (put), take (took), see (saw).

Don't do that! Let's go! Stop it! What's happening?

Unit 3: cave, jewel, men; dark, first, gold, quiet, scared; everywhere, left, right, round and round; bump (-ed), run, shine, sleep, stop (stopped), wake up.

Be quiet! I don't know. Quick! Sshh! You're right!

Unit 4: cow, cloud, desert, dust, future, ice, past, present, wind, yak; cold, dry, flat, hot, long, rocky, sandy; with a bump, far away, nearer and nearer; land (-ed);

Brrr!

Unit 5: afternoon, camel, house, man, neck, present, [nb "present" = "gift" here – different from Unit 4] rock, round, tent, world; beautiful, cosy, fast, next, warm, young; climb (-ed), find (found), get (got) off, leave, look after, stay (-ed).

Unit 6: animal, elephant, mammoth, forest, path, spaceship, tiger, woman; better, dangerous, exciting, frightened, frightening, silver, surprised, worse; run away, appear (-ed).

It's OK. Phew! What's the matter?

Unit 7: corner, cockerel, crowd, duck, field, friend, hot air balloon, France, passengers, people, sheep, sky, sun, year; famous, funny; catch, disappear (-ed), fall, fly, rise.

Go on! Really? There it goes! Wonderful! You can do it!

Unit 8: flight, pirate, sailing ship, sea, stranger; bumpy, careful, short; slowly, quietly; catch (caught), fly (flew), look for, start (-ed), take (tor off, turn (-ed), run (ran).

Be quiet! Come here! Hooray! Perhaps. .u. Well done!

Unit 9: family, home; here, just in time, there; bang (-ed), shout (-ed), shut, travel, want.

Yes, of course.

Unit 10: boy, journey, pilot; scary, silly; arrive (-d), dance, hunt, meet (met), ride, show (-ed), swing, talk.

Unit 11: branch, coral, diving suit, fault, fish, fun, sea snake, shark, splash, starfish, water; clear, lost, tiny, worried; at once, together; follow (-ed), put (put) on, swim (swam), worry.

I don't believe it! Sorry!

Unit 12: chest, coins, crab, wreck; can (could).

Don't worry! There you are!

Unit 13: basket, bus, car, carriage, chocolate, cold, flask, flower, girl, horse, juice, London, lorry, seller; busy, delicious, hungry, thirsty; far away; cross (-ed), give (gave), need (-ed), sell, shiver, speak (spoke), thank (-ed).

Are you all right? Here it is! Here you are! Oh dear! You're welcome.

Unit 14: back, chariot, front, race, Rome, stadium; impossible; brightly; cheer, clap, notice (-ed), pull, race, wait, watch.

I have no idea. Well, well, well!

Unit 15: bird, colour, crystal, ice cream, net, rainbow, tree; hang, pick (-ed), slip (slipped), fall (fell).

Be careful!

Unit 16: rope; naughty, fine, yummy; always, never, sometimes; ask (-ed), swing, hold, lie, throw (threw).

All right.

Unit 17: garden, face, fountain, orange, place, pool, trunk; clever; at last; reach (-ed) up.

Unit 18: cushion, keyhole, middle, palace, table; ready; walk (-ed).